The Military History of World War II
Volume 7

THE AIR WAR IN THE WEST
June 1941 – April 1945

THE MILITARY HISTORY OF WORLD WAR II

Vol. 1 — European Land Battles: 1939-1943
Vol. 2 — European Land Battles: 1944-1945
Vol. 3 — Land Battles: North Africa, Sicily, and Italy
Vol. 4 — The Naval War in the West: The Raiders
Vol. 5 — The Naval War in the West: The Wolf Packs
Vol. 6 — The Air War in the West: September 1939-May 1941
Vol. 7 — The Air War in the West: June 1941-April 1945

Forthcoming:
Vol. 8 — Asiatic Land Battles: Expansion of Japan in Asia
Vol. 9 — Asiatic Land Battles: Japanese Ambitions in the Pacific
Vol. 10 — Asiatic Land Battles: Allied Victories in China and
        Burma
Vol. 11 — The Naval War in the Pacific: Rising Sun of Nippon
Vol. 12 — The Naval War in the Pacific: On to Tokyo
Vol. 13 — The Air War in the Pacific: Air Power Leads the Way
Vol. 14 — The Air War in the Pacific: Victory in the Air
Vol. 15 — The Resistance
Vol. 16 — World War II Summary

The Military History of World War II: Volume 7

THE AIR WAR IN THE WEST
June 1941 – April 1945

by Trevor Nevitt Dupuy
COL., U.S. ARMY, RET.

FRANKLIN WATTS, INC.
575 Lexington Avenue • New York 22

TO MARY

Library of Congress Catalog Card Number: 63-9799
Copyright © 1963 by Franklin Watts, Inc.
Printed in the United States of America
by Polygraphic Company of America

1   2   3   4   5   6   7

Contents

THE AIR WAR IN EASTERN EUROPE   1

  The Germans Invade Russia, 1
  Moscow and Stalingrad, 4
  Final Air Operations in the East, 6

AIR LABORATORY IN NORTH AFRICA   7

  Air Power in the Western Desert, 7
  Developing a New Air-Ground Doctrine, 10
  Proof in Tunisia, 13

THE ALLIED STRATEGIC AIR OFFENSIVE   19

  British Retaliation Against Germany, 19
  The Arrival of the American Bombers, 23
  The Combined Bomber Offensive, 26
  Ploesti, 27
  The Schweinfurt Lesson, 32
  The Big Week, 34

AIR POWER AND THE NORMANDY INVASION   36

  Operation OVERLORD, 36
  The Role of Strategic Air Power, 41
  Air Support Over the Beaches, 43

AIR WAR OVER WESTERN EUROPE   48

  Breakout from Normandy, 48
  The V-Bombs, 49
  Air-Ground Cooperation, 56

THE DESTRUCTION OF THE *Luftwaffe*   61

  Climax of the Strategic Air Offensive, 61
  The Luftwaffe's *Last Efforts*, 63

INDEX   65

The Air War in Eastern Europe

The Germans Invade Russia

AFTER THE GERMANS had been defeated in the Battle of Britain, Hitler had decided to soften up the English people by the continuous night terror bombings of the "blitz," while at the same time his submarines cut off England's food supply and prevented raw materials from reaching Britain's factories. He had figured that England would then be ripe for conquest by 1942.

Meanwhile, he had decided, he would conquer Russia. The impressive *blitzkrieg* victories his forces had won in Poland, Norway, western Europe, and the Balkans had convinced him that the *Luftwaffe* and the *Wehrmacht*, working together, were unbeatable. He was sure that they could defeat the Red Army and the Soviet air force without any trouble.

In May and June, 1941, Hitler assembled three great army groups, totaling about two million men, along the western borders of Soviet Russia in eastern Europe. In support of them were three *Luftwaffe* air fleets; in the north was the First Air Fleet, under General Alfred Keller; in the center was the Second Air Fleet, commanded by Field Marshal Albert Kesselring; and the Fourth Air Fleet, under General Alexander Loehr, supported the Southern Army Group. Together, these three air fleets included more than three thousand operational combat aircraft.

Hitler had planned to start the invasion of Russia at the beginning of June, but he had had to wait until the Fourth Air Fleet could be moved from Crete and Greece. At last, before dawn on June 22, the German air and ground forces struck Russia in a surprise *blitzkrieg* like those that had been so successful before.

1

The Soviet air force consisted of about eight thousand planes, and more than half of them were ready for battle in western Russia. But only a few of these aircraft were as good as the *Luftwaffe* planes. Russian pilots were not as well trained as the Germans, and they did not have the combat experience of the veteran invaders.

Despite the greater numbers of the Russian ground and air forces, the *Luftwaffe* and the *Wehrmacht* quickly proved their superiority. The Germans destroyed great numbers of Russian planes on the

Russian planes in flight.

ground, and shot down many more in air battles over the fighting front. By the beginning of July, the *Luftwaffe* had established complete aerial superiority in western Russia and could devote itself to giving effective ground support to the German armies.

During the summer and fall, the German invaders swept deep into Russia, destroying many Russian armies and capturing tremendous numbers of prisoners. As in the earlier campaigns, the assistance of *Luftwaffe* dive bombers and strafing fighter planes helped the German ground forces to win victory after victory. Yet despite their terrible losses, the Russians were able to bring reserves from eastern Russia and Siberia, and to raise new armies from their great population. At the same time, many German tanks and airplanes were wearing out from continuous moving and fighting, and the German airmen were getting very tired. And as the German forces penetrated deeper and deeper into Russia, it became more difficult to bring up enough food, ammunition, and gasoline to keep them supplied.

Hitler himself added to the problems of his armed forces in Russia by making some very serious mistakes. By this time he believed he was a military genius. He had been so certain of the superiority of German ground and air forces that he had been confident the Russians would be completely defeated before the end of the summer. For this reason he had not allowed his generals to assemble winter clothes for the troops, or winter oil and grease for the airplanes, tanks, and trucks. He had failed to consider how difficult it would be for his armies and air fleets to move and fight over the vast distances of Russia. Hitler's changing orders to his military commanders still further slowed down the advance. He had not realized that the Russians would be able to assemble new armies to defend their country after the frontline forces had been destroyed.

Moscow and Stalingrad

THE EXHAUSTED, FREEZING GERMAN ARMIES were brought to a halt in early December, just outside of Moscow. The warmly dressed Russian troops counterattacked and threw back the lightly clad Germans. For a while it seemed as though the German armies would collapse. Then, despite the terrible weather, the *Luftwaffe* made a supreme effort. German dive bombers and fighters struck time and again at the Russians, slowing their advance and giving the *Wehrmacht* time to recover from panic and defeat. By superior skill and leadership the Germans then halted the Russian counteroffensive, and the two great armies entrenched themselves. During the rest of the winter they attempted to recover from the frightful losses they had both suffered during the long campaign.

In the summer of 1942, the *Wehrmacht*, now rested, again struck powerful blows against the Russians. Again they came close to victory. But the Russians by now had learned a number of valuable lessons from the Germans, and they had received many tanks, weapons, and airplanes from Britain and America. Although the *Luftwaffe* was still far superior to the Russian air force, it did not have enough planes and pilots to keep control of the skies along the entire two-thousand-mile battlefront. Russian bombers and fighters began to strike back in areas where German air power was weak. At night, Soviet planes carried supplies and weapons to Russian resistance fighters in the vast regions behind the German lines.

The story of the previous year was repeated: Hitler's mistakes, combined with the stubborn resistance of the Russians, finally halted the German drive. In November, at Stalingrad, the Red Army repulsed attack after attack by the Germans. Finally it surrounded the entire German Sixth Army.

One of the thirty-nine Hurricane fighter planes supplied by Britain to Russia in the summer of 1941. A British crew briefs Russian airmen on the plane's operation.

The *Luftwaffe* came immediately to the assistance of the trapped army. While German combat planes bombarded and strafed the Russian entrenchments, German transport aircraft flew in great quantities of food and ammunition. Before long the surrounded German troops were ready to fight their way out of the Russian trap. But Hitler insisted that they must not retreat one step from Stalingrad. While the German generals tried to persuade him to change his orders, the Russians brought in tremendous ground and air reinforcements to strengthen their encircling siege lines. On February 2, 1943, the Sixth Army was forced to surrender. This was the beginning of the end for Adolf Hitler.

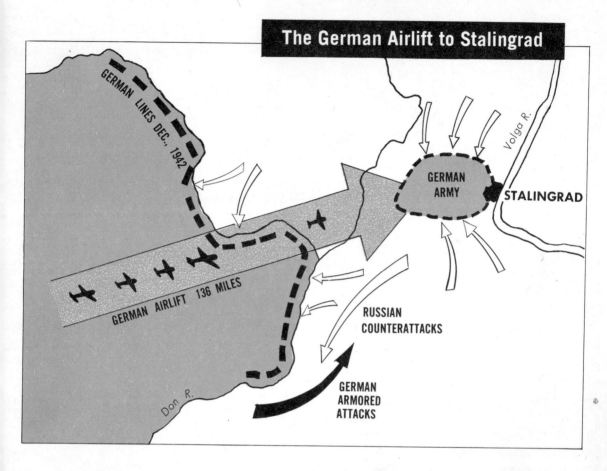

GERMAN LINES DEC., 1942

GERMAN AIRLIFT 136 MILES

GERMAN
ARMY

STALINGRAD

Volga R.

RUSSIAN
COUNTERATTACKS

GERMAN
ARMORED
ATTACKS

Don R.

Final Air Operations in the East

IN 1943 AND 1944 the Russian armies slowly but surely drove back
the Germans. Because the *Luftwaffe* had to keep its strongest forces
in western Europe to oppose the American and British air assaults,
German air strength dwindled on the eastern front. At the same

6

time, Russian air strength steadily increased. Russian factories built more planes, and great numbers of aircraft and other lend-lease supplies from Britain and America were delivered to the Russians.

Until late in 1944, despite growing Russian air strength, the *Luftwaffe* was always able to gain local air superiority at any point where it managed to assemble enough strength to challenge the Soviets. German planes and German pilots were still better than Russian planes and pilots. German bombers made a few long-range attacks on Moscow and other Russian manufacturing and transportation centers, while at the same time German defensive fighters repulsed most Russian attempts to bomb Germany. And whenever the *Wehrmacht* made a counterattack against the Russian advance, *Luftwaffe* planes carried out fierce ground strikes against the Soviet troops.

By 1945, however, the *Luftwaffe* had fought and lost a series of tremendous battles with the air forces of America and Britain in western Europe. Germany no longer had planes to replace those lost on the eastern front. German planes were now so outnumbered in Russia that they could offer no further effective opposition to the Russian air force. Russian planes had complete control of the skies over eastern Germany, and were helping their tremendous ground armies in the final massive attacks against Berlin.

Air Laboratory in North Africa

Air Power in the Western Desert

IN THE EARLY MONTHS OF 1941, the British had reinforced the Royal Air Force units in the Middle East with Spitfires, Hurricanes, and aircraft bought in America. At this time, Hitler was also increasing

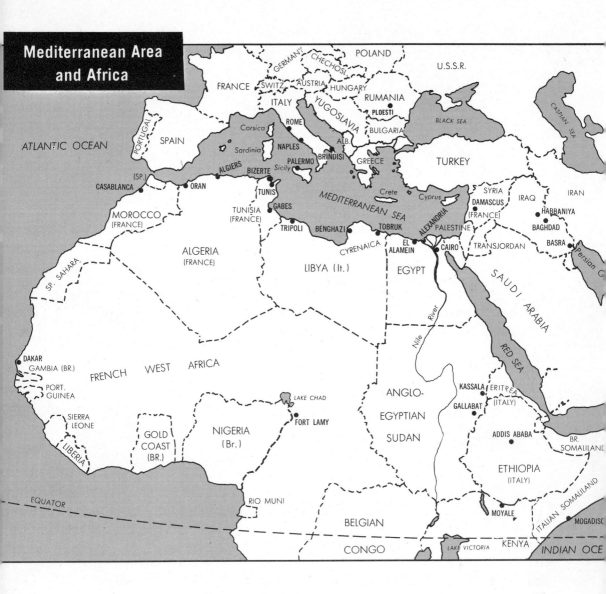

Mediterranean Area and Africa

ATLANTIC OCEAN

GERMANY
CHECHOSL.
POLAND
U.S.S.R.
FRANCE
SWITZ
AUSTRIA
HUNGARY
ITALY
RUMANIA
PLOESTI
YUGOSLAVIA
BULGARIA
BLACK SEA
CASPIAN SEA
Corsica
ROME
ALB.
GREECE
TURKEY
PORTUGAL
SPAIN
Sardinia
NAPLES
BRINDISI
PALERMO
Sicily
ALGIERS
BIZERTE
Crete
Cyprus
SYRIA
IRAQ
IRAN
CASABLANCA
(SP.)
ORAN
TUNIS
MEDITERRANEAN SEA
DAMASCUS
HABBANIYA
GABES
(FRANCE)
ALEXANDRIA
BAGHDAD
MOROCCO
(FRANCE)
TUNISIA
(FRANCE)
TRIPOLI
BENGHAZI
TOBRUK
PALESTINE
BASRA
Persian G.
EL
CYRENAICA
ALAMEIN
CAIRO
TRANSJORDAN
ALGERIA
(FRANCE)
LIBYA (It.)
EGYPT
SAUDI ARABIA
SP. SAHARA
Nile River
RED SEA
DAKAR
GAMBIA (BR.)
PORT.
GUINEA
FRENCH
WEST
AFRICA
KASSALA
ERITREA
(ITALY)
GALLABAT
SIERRA
LEONE
Lake Chad
ANGLO-
EGYPTIAN
SUDAN
ADDIS ABABA
BR.
SOMALILAND
LIBERIA
GOLD
COAST
(BR.)
NIGERIA
(Br.)
FORT LAMY
ETHIOPIA
(ITALY)
EQUATOR
RIO MUNI
MOYALE
ITALIAN SOMALILAND
MOGADISC
BELGIAN
KENYA
INDIAN OCE
CONGO
Lake Victoria

8

his air force in the Mediterranean area. He had shifted two of his air fleets from northern and western Europe to attack Malta and to support the German invasion of the Balkans. He had also sent a large number of Messerschmitt fighters and Stuka dive bombers to help General Erwin Rommel try to capture the Suez Canal from the British.

Only one of these three German air offensives was completely successful. In the Balkans the *Luftwaffe* had driven the Royal Air Force first from Greece and then from Crete. In the operations against Malta, the Germans and Italians had obtained air superiority and put the British flyers on the defensive, but they had never succeeded in completely eliminating the Royal Air Force from the island.

In North Africa, the *Luftwaffe* had gained control of the air over the immediate battle lines, and had been of great help to the *Afrika Korps* during Rommel's successful offensive of April and May, 1941. But the Germans had been less successful in their efforts to destroy British air bases in Egypt. The British army had held the besieged seaport of Tobruk despite persistent German dive-bombing and strafing attacks. This had prevented Rommel from moving his air bases east of Tobruk, where he would have been within closer striking distance of the Royal Air Force's Egyptian airfields.

In the following months, most of Hitler's attention had been devoted to operations in Russia, and he had sent few air or ground reinforcements to Rommel. But the British had continued to build up their strength in Egypt. By the late months of 1941, the Royal Air Force's Desert Air Force had regained air superiority over the Western Desert. The Germans, however, had managed to protect their airfields in Libya so that they could still provide powerful support to Rommel in quick hit-and-run attacks.

During 1942, the British had still further increased their superiority in the air in North Africa, but they had never completely overwhelmed Rommel's *Luftwaffe* contingent. And despite British control of the skies, Rommel had won a great many ground victories.

Developing a New Air-Ground Doctrine

THE SENIOR ROYAL AIR FORCE OFFICER in the Middle East in 1942 was Air Vice Marshal Arthur W. Tedder. Under him, the immediate commander of the Desert Air Force was Air Vice Marshal Arthur Coningham. Tedder and Coningham, working in close coordination with the British ground force commanders, devoted much of their time and attention to testing old and new theories for air support to land armies.

The result of these tests and experiments was the development of a complete doctrine (method of operation) for air-ground co-operation. The effectiveness of this doctrine in the Western Desert was thoroughly proven when Coningham's Desert Air Force worked closely with General Bernard L. Montgomery's Eighth Army in winning a decisive victory over Rommel at the Battle of El Alamein.

This doctrine was so carefully worked out that it is still the standard for air-ground warfare. It was a simple system of operations, and its three principal elements did not appear to be much different from the doctrine which the *Luftwaffe* had used in its successful co-operation with the *Wehrmacht* in Poland, France, and the Balkans.

The first of these basic elements of the Tedder-Coningham-Montgomery doctrine was that the first and principal mission of the air forces must be to gain air superiority. Therefore, before they could give much, or any, direct support to the ground troops, they must defeat the enemy's air force in the sky and destroy or seriously damage his bases on the ground.

*A British Halifax bomber being made ready to bomb Rommel's positions in the
Western Desert.*

IMPERIAL WAR MUSEUM, LONDON

11

Second, after air superiority had been gained, the air force could best help the ground army by "isolating the battlefield." This meant that the next important task for the air units would be to cut road and railroad lines and destroy supply bases so that the enemy could not send reinforcements or supplies to his ground combat forces.

Third, and less important than gaining air superiority or isolating the battlefields, the air force would offer direct support to the army by bombing and strafing the enemy's frontline troops.

The principal difference between the British method of operation and the one the Germans had been using, and the Americans, Russians, and Japanese were still using, was in the way the air units were controlled. The German method had been to place each unit under the control of the forces it supported. But this method was not very effective when the opposing air force concentrated large numbers of planes in one area. When the various air units were scattered along the line, there was always the possibility that they could be overwhelmed one at a time by such a concentrated attack before they could be regrouped.

The British, therefore, decided that all air units should be kept under one central control — that of the senior Royal Air Force commander. This meant that once air superiority had been obtained, it would still be easy for the commander to send separate air units to support various armies. The great value of the British method lay in the ability of the central command to quickly gather all air units together to fight as a team if the enemy threatened Allied air superiority in one area by an unexpected concentration of planes. And this same system of central command made it easier for the Royal Air Force commander to concentrate superior forces to bomb and strafe enemy ground forces in support of main British attacks.

The British found this system very satisfactory, but when the

United States entered the war, many American ground soldiers were unwilling to accept it. They were afraid it would keep them from getting as much air support as they needed, at the time when they needed it. In the early days of the war, the Americans stuck to the system so successfully used by the *Luftwaffe* in its *blitzkrieg* campaigns.

Proof in Tunisia

ON NOVEMBER 8, 1942, combined British and American forces under General Dwight D. Eisenhower made amphibious landings in Algiers and Oran in French Algeria, and at Casablanca in French Morocco. The Vichy-French resisted strongly, but not for long. On November 10 and 11 they surrendered. Eisenhower immediately ordered an advance toward Tunisia to cut off Field Marshal Rommel's retreat from El Alamein.

As early as November 9, the Germans had realized that the Allied landings constituted a serious threat to German forces in North Africa. The *Luftwaffe* had at once begun an emergency airlift of soldiers from Italy to Tunisia.

Soon after this British and American planes dropped paratroops to seize airfields along the border of Tunisia and Algeria. The troops that had landed at Oran and Algiers hurried along the coast to join the paratroopers, while Allied transport planes brought in supplies to the captured airfields. By the end of November, the Allies were advancing rapidly toward the cities of Bizerte and Tunis, hoping to seize them before the German airlift could bring in enough troops for effective defense. On December 1, Allied troops were within forty miles of Tunis.

Then, that very day, General D. J. von Arnim, supported by

Luftwaffe dive bombers, attacked westward from Tunis and drove the advancing Allied units back. Although the German ground forces were outnumbered, the excellent support they received from the *Luftwaffe* helped them to keep the Allies from advancing any farther. By the middle of December, the ground troops of both sides were entrenching along a line running southward through central Tunisia.

B-24 flight and ground crews of the 8th Bomber Command lived in the desert for three months, during which time their diet consisted of Spam and dehydrated cabbage. U.S. AIR FORCE PHOTO

Royal Air Force pilots rush to answer an alert in the Western Desert.

For two months there was a stalemate in Tunisia while both sides built up their strength. Then, as January came to a close, Rommel reached southeastern Tunisia. His long retreat from El Alamein was ended. He established a strong defensive position at Mareth and prepared to attack the Americans in southwestern Tunisia.

On February 14, 1943, Rommel began a carefully planned, joint air and ground attack against the Americans who were holding the Allied line from Faid to El Guettar. For the first time the American troops faced a *blitzkrieg* attack, and they fell back in confusion. The American air units supporting the ground defenders were overwhelmed by the concentration of all available German planes.

As his troops retreated back toward Kasserine Pass, American Major General Lloyd Fredendall called for additional air support from General Eisenhower's headquarters at Algiers. Since the Americans were using their old system of divided air force control, all the Allied air units had been attached individually to ground forces elsewhere along the front, and they were all busy carrying out assigned missions. There were no planes available to help the American ground soldiers who were being swept back through Kasserine Pass by the Germans.

Finally the American troops began to recover from their confusion. They slowed down the German advance, which was now approaching the main Allied base at Tebessa in eastern Algeria. Then, as soon as Eisenhower was able to shift air units from other parts of the front, American planes began to offer more resistance to the *Luftwaffe*. On February 22, barely twenty miles from Tebessa, the German advance was halted. By this time the Allies had assembled an overwhelming number of planes in the region and had regained air superiority. Rommel now knew he could not take Tebessa, so he withdrew to his original positions. Meanwhile, he had taught the Americans what *blitzkrieg* really meant.

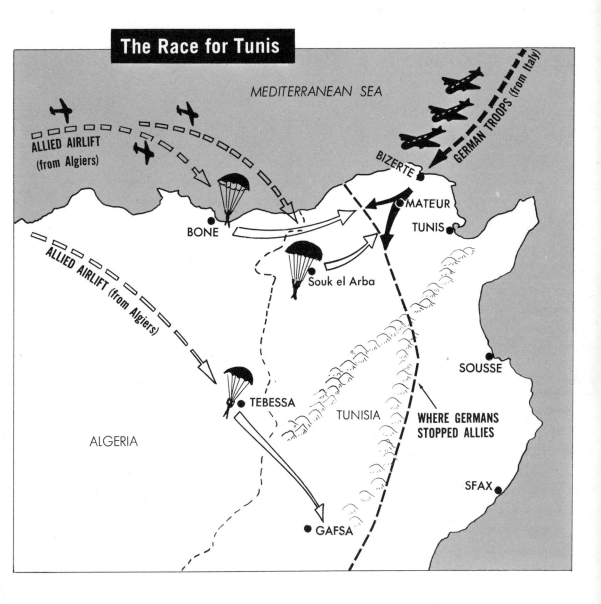

The Race for Tunis

MEDITERRANEAN SEA

GERMAN TROOPS (from Italy)

ALLIED AIRLIFT
(from Algiers)

BIZERTE

MATEUR

BONE

TUNIS

Souk el Arba

ALLIED AIRLIFT (from Algiers)

SOUSSE

TEBESSA

TUNISIA

WHERE GERMANS
STOPPED ALLIES

ALGERIA

SFAX

GAFSA

A Douglas C-47 flies over the pyramids in Egypt.

Rommel had also taught the Americans that prompt air support to ground troops could best be given with the British system of centralized control. As a result, General Eisenhower completely reorganized his air command arrangements. Air Marshal Tedder was placed in overall control of all Allied air forces in the Mediterranean area, under Eisenhower. From then until the end of the war, the Americans as well as the British used the doctrine of air-ground cooperation which Tedder and Coningham had worked out in the Western Desert.

18

The Allied Strategic Air Offensive

British Retaliation Against Germany

As EARLY AS THE SUMMER OF 1940, the Royal Air Force's Bomber Command had begun to attack targets in Germany in retaliation for the damage the *Luftwaffe* was doing in England during the Battle of Britain. It was a British raid on Berlin that had been partly re-

Royal Air Force pilots study a map in preparation for a raid over Germany.

sponsible for the mistake Hitler and Goering had made in ordering the all-out assault on London in September, 1940.

Because there were no British bases between England and Germany, the Royal Air Force bombers had been forced to fly longer distances than the German planes, which had been able to raid Britain from France and the Low Countries. This had meant that the British planes had to carry more gasoline than the *Luftwaffe* planes and, consequently, smaller bombloads. Also, the British had not had as many bombers as the Germans, and so the Royal Air Force's raids had been less damaging to Germany than the *Luftwaffe*'s had been to England. Nevertheless, the British people had found some satisfaction in knowing that the Germans were taking some of the same kind of punishment they were giving England, and that the German people were learning that the Nazis could not keep their promise to prevent any enemy bombs from striking Germany.

Giant Wurzburg German radar antennae.

IMPERIAL WAR MUSEUM, LONDON

This huge searchlight helped to protect Berlin against air attack.

    The German air defenses had been strong. Although neither their radar warning nets nor their ground-control system had equaled those of the British, their defensive fighter units had been excellent, and their antiaircraft guns had been accurate. For this reason the Royal Air Force leaders had decided not to try to raid Germany by day, when their planes could be easily spotted and shot down. Instead they developed a night bombing system.

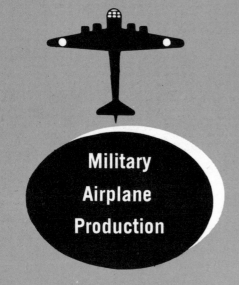

Military Airplane Production

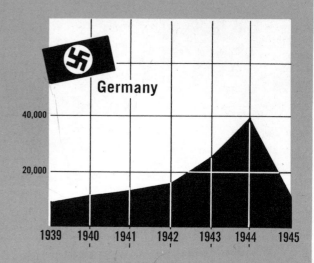

Germany

40,000

20,000

1939 1940 1941 1942 1943 1944 1945

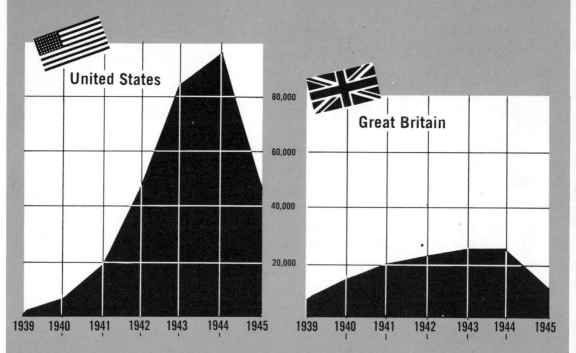

United States

80,000

60,000

40,000

20,000

1939 1940 1941 1942 1943 1944 1945

Great Britain

20,000

1939 1940 1941 1942 1943 1944 1945

After the Royal Air Force had won the Battle of Britain, the Chief of Staff of the Royal Air Force, Air Chief Marshal Sir Charles Portal, decided to cut down on the number of fighter planes being built in England, and to concentrate on building more bombers. Portal and Prime Minister Churchill were determined that the war should be brought home to the German people as it had already been brought home to the British. During 1941 and 1942 the strength of Bomber Command grew steadily, and the night blows against German industrial cities and other targets grew heavier. On the night of May 30-31, 1942, Bomber Command made the first 1,000-plane raid against Germany in an attack against the railroad marshaling yards at Cologne.

Germany was now suffering more damage from Royal Air Force raids than the *Luftwaffe* had inflicted on England during the blitz. Hitler was beginning to realize what a terrible mistake he had made by attacking Russia before he had defeated Britain.

The Arrival of the American Bombers

THE UNITED STATES had entered World War II in December, 1941, as a result of the Japanese attack on Pearl Harbor. The British and American military leaders, with the approval of President Roosevelt and Prime Minister Churchill, had at that time decided that Germany was a more dangerous enemy than Japan, and so they had agreed to try to defeat Germany as quickly as possible. One of their first efforts would be a tremendous bombing offensive to destroy Germany's war industries.

General Henry H. Arnold, commander of the United States Army Air Forces, had understood why the British were making their raids against Germany by night, but he and other American airmen knew that daylight bombing was more accurate. They believed that they had the means to stage such daylight raids, without serious losses, and thus help to hasten the defeat of Germany.

These men had had firm basis for their belief. The United States had developed two new, fast types of bombers, equipped with enough machine guns and armor protection to be able to trade blows with German fighters. One of these bombers — the B-17 — because of its armament, had been nicknamed the "Flying Fortress." The other — the B-24 — almost as well protected, had been called "Liberator." In addition to these two bombers, the Americans had developed the best bombsight in the world. It would enable them to make very accurate daylight strikes.

At the time of Pearl Harbor, the United States had not built many B-17's or B-24's, so it was several months before American bombing units could be sent to England. Meanwhile, the Royal Air Force continued its night raids.

In July, 1942, the first American bombers arrived in England. They were organized as the United States Eighth Air Force, under the command of Lieutenant General Carl Spaatz. Spaatz and Air Marshal Sir Arthur T. Harris, commanding Bomber Command, worked out an understanding in which the Royal Air Force would bomb targets on the Continent at night, while the U.S. Army Air Force would do its bombing in daylight. The first American air raid was carried out on August 17, 1942, against the railroad marshaling yards at Rouen, in occupied France.

The Eighth Air Force had only a few planes to start with, and it grew very slowly because other long-range air forces — the Ninth and Twelfth — were being created at the same time in North Africa. So for the first few months of its existence, the Eighth Air Force made only a few, small raids, mostly for training purposes, against

U.S. AIR FORCE PHOTO

B-24 Liberators fly over the Adriatic on their way to bomb targets in Italy.

A B-17 in North Africa.

U.S. ARMY PHOTOGRAPH

Three of the Eighth Air Force's leaders meet in England during the command's strategic aerial bombardment of Nazi Europe. Facing the camera, left to right, are Generals Carl A. Spaatz, James Doolittle, and William Kepner.

U.S. AIR FORCE PHOTO

military targets in France. Its first big raid against Germany came on January 27, 1943, when it attacked German submarine pens at Wilhelmshaven. Not until June, 1943, were American striking forces strong enough to really begin the long-planned Combined Bomber Offensive against Germany.

The Combined Bomber Offensive

THE BRITISH AND AMERICAN air attacks against Germany had two principal objectives. The first of these was to destroy or weaken the defensive fighter forces of the *Luftwaffe* so as to gain control of the

26

air over Germany. This would be done in two ways: first, by daylight air battles between the German fighters and the B-17's and B-24's; second, by making German aircraft factories the first and most important targets for the Royal Air Force and U.S. Army Air Force raids.

As soon as the Allies had air superiority over Germany, the bombing attacks would be expanded to include critical portions of the German war industry. This would make it increasingly difficult for the Germans to provide planes, tanks, weapons, and other supplies to their widely spread fighting forces. Long-range bombing attacks could only have an indirect effect on actual battlefield — or "tactical" — operations. But, by making it more difficult for Germany to continue the war, these far-reaching air blows naturally contributed to the overall Allied strategy of the war. And so the long-range strikes of the Combined Bomber Offensive were called "strategic" air operations.

Ploesti

ONE OF THE FIRST and most dramatic of the United States Air Force's long-range strategic air strikes came on August 1, 1943. It was not against Germany, but it was against a target of great importance to the Germans: the oil refineries at Ploesti, Romania. These refineries furnished Germany with more than three million tons of oil and gasoline each year. This included most of the fuel for German planes and tanks.

In the summer of 1943, the American air leaders decided to make a surprise bombing raid on Ploesti from their bases in North Africa. In addition to the B-24 bombers of the Ninth Air Force already in North Africa, several units of the Eighth Air Force were flown in from England to bases near Benghazi, in Libya.

On August 1, 178 B-24's took off from these bases, and headed for

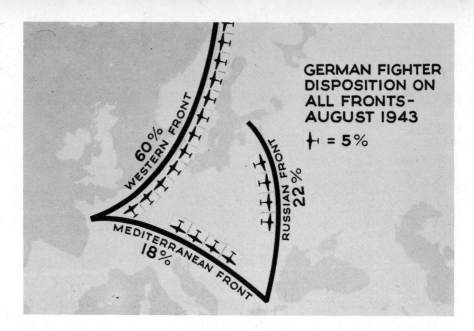

GERMAN FIGHTER
DISPOSITION ON
ALL FRONTS—
AUGUST 1943

✈ = 5%

WESTERN FRONT 60%

RUSSIAN FRONT 22%

MEDITERRANEAN FRONT 18%

Ploesti, which was about one thousand miles away. Never before had a bombing raid been conducted over so great a distance. The Americans had been careful to keep the plans secret, and they were sure that the Germans would not expect such an attack.

But the American commanders had underrated German alertness and efficiency. German radar sets in Greece, Bulgaria, and Romania soon revealed the great air armada on their screens. The formidable antiaircraft defenses at Ploesti were warned of the approach of the American bombers.

To confuse the Germans, and to make it difficult for them to use their long-range, high-altitude, antiaircraft guns, the American planes made a low-level bombing attack. When they reached Ploesti they barely cleared the tops of trees and buildings. Many of the planes actually flew below and between the tops of the high refinery chimneys. But the Germans were ready for them. Yet even though some of the leading planes were shot down, this did little to discourage the others. Most of them came in for their bombing runs without hesitation.

This shot gives a vivid idea of how low the B-24's flew in bombing the Ploesti oil refineries.

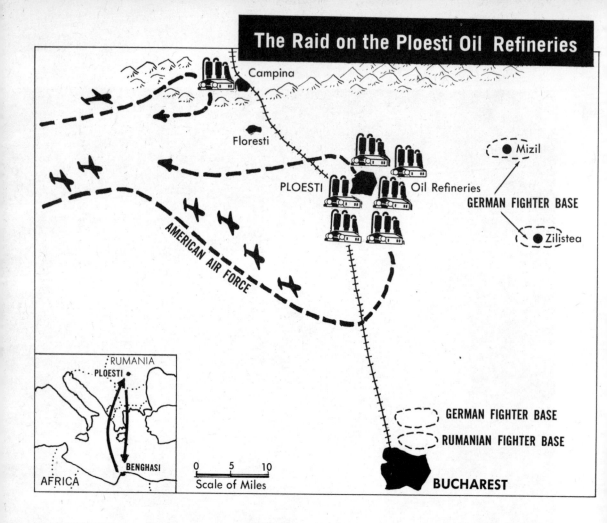

The Raid on the Ploesti Oil Refineries

Campina

Floresti

Mizil

PLOESTI   Oil Refineries

GERMAN FIGHTER BASE

Zilistea

AMERICAN AIR FORCE

RUMANIA

PLOESTI

GERMAN FIGHTER BASE

RUMANIAN FIGHTER BASE

BENGHASI

AFRICA

0   5   10
Scale of Miles

BUCHAREST

Clouds of smoke from exploding oil tanks and destroyed planes were soon rolling over Ploesti. Thousands of antiaircraft shells flashed brilliantly in the murk and gloom that hung over the refineries. Still the American planes came in. Sometimes they could see their targets a few feet below them; sometimes they had to drop their bombs into the smoke clouds, hoping they would have some effect.

Captured German films showing the burning Ploesti refineries during the American attack.

Fifty-six of the attacking planes were shot down, and many more were damaged. Most of the hits were made by German antiaircraft guns, though a few German fighter planes had also attacked the American bombers. Because they had destroyed many buildings, and because of the amount of smoke they had seen stirred up by their explosions, the Americans thought they had knocked out the refineries. Actually, the damage was superficial. Most of the smoke had come from storage tanks, while the big refineries themselves had not suffered as severely as the Americans believed. In a few days, German engineers had the plants running again at full capacity. The Ploesti raid had been a brave undertaking, but it had cost the Americans more than it was worth.

The Schweinfurt Lesson

As THEY INCREASED THE SCALE of their attacks against Germany, American air commanders soon found that they had underrated the capabilities of the *Luftwaffe* fighter pilots. Many B-17's and B-24's were being shot down, while German losses were not very heavy. The deeper the Americans went into Germany, the greater were their losses, because the German planes, fighting closer to their own bases, had more time to attack them.

In October, 1943, the Americans decided to risk heavy losses in an attack against the large ball-bearing factory at Schweinfurt. This factory provided ball bearings for practically all of the German tank and airplane factories. If it could be knocked out, German production of tanks and planes would be greatly reduced.

The first raid against Schweinfurt caught the Germans by surprise. The factory was seriously damaged, while the attacking American bombers suffered relatively small losses. Nevertheless, the factory

The 100th Bombardment Group bombs Schweinfurt, Germany.

U.S. AIR FORCE PHOTO

was able to go on producing ball bearings, even though it did so at a reduced rate.

On October 14, 1943, the Eighth Air Force sent nearly three hundred bombers on a second raid against Schweinfurt. This time the German fighters were ready and waiting. They shot down sixty of the attacking American planes, but lost very few of their own. The ball-bearing factory suffered only slightly more damage than it had suffered in the first raid.

The experience at Schweinfurt proved to the Americans that their bombers could not penetrate deep into Germany without fighter-plane escorts. Neither the Americans nor the British had enough long-range fighters at that time to protect the American bombers, so for several months the Americans limited their daylight bombing to targets in occupied countries or western Germany. Meanwhile, American factories worked overtime to turn out large numbers of the new P-51 "Mustang" fighters, which would have enough range to go into the heart of Germany with the bombers.

The Big Week

BY THE BEGINNING OF 1944, there were enough P-51's in England to enable the American Eighth Air Force to renew its raids into central Germany. Hermann Goering refused to believe that there were any fighter planes in the world that could fly that far and still be fast enough and maneuverable enough to fight on even terms with his Messerschmitts. He finally believed it when four P-51's chased the *Luftwaffe* fighter chief, Lieutenant General Adolf Galland, all the way from western Germany to Berlin.

Between February 20 and 25, 1944, the bombers of the American Eighth Air Force and the Italian-based Fifteenth Air Force ranged

P-51 Mustang fighters of the Fifteenth Air Force fly over the Alps in a practice formation.

all over Germany accompanied by their escort fighters. Their main targets were aircraft factories, but they also attacked the ball-bearing plant at Schweinfurt; this time only eleven planes were lost out of the 266 attacking Schweinfurt. During these six days the Americans shot down several hundred German fighters, and seriously crippled the German aircraft industry.

One result of these Allied raids was that Goering ordered his defensive fighters to avoid combat with the P-51's, and to attack

American bombers only when there were no fighters nearby. One *Luftwaffe* officer remarked with bitter humor that the safest flying in the world was that of an "American fighter over Germany." After a slow start, the American daylight bombing raids were now doing more damage to German industry than the Royal Air Force night attacks.

Air Power and the Normandy Invasion

Operation OVERLORD

IN JANUARY, 1943, President Roosevelt and Prime Minister Churchill met with their top military advisers, the Combined Chiefs of Staff, at Casablanca, Morocco. There the Allied leaders agreed to invade German-occupied western Europe in the spring of 1944. Later this invasion plan was given the code name of Operation OVERLORD. In December, 1943, General Eisenhower was appointed Supreme Allied Commander of the great land, sea, and air forces which were gathering in England for the invasion.

To help him plan and control the gigantic operation, Eisenhower selected as his deputy commander British Air Chief Marshal Tedder, who had coordinated air and ground operations in the fighting in Tunisia, Sicily, and Italy. Early in January, 1944, Eisenhower, accompanied by Tedder, flew from North Africa to England to take over his new command.

During the next four months Eisenhower, Tedder, and the British and American officers of their staff completed the complicated plans for Operation OVERLORD. The invasion was scheduled for early June, when Allied naval forces were to carry more than one million British and American ground soldiers across the English Channel to

President Franklin Delano Roosevelt with Prime Minister Winston Churchill at the Casablanca Conference.

37

make an amphibious landing on the coast of Normandy, in France.

Eisenhower and his officers knew that OVERLORD could not be successful unless the U.S. Army Air Force and the Royal Air Force could first smash the *Luftwaffe*. The Allied problem was like that which had faced the Germans in the summer of 1940, when they were planning to invade England. Unless the invaders had complete control of the skies over the Channel and its nearby shores, the defending air and naval forces might sink so many ships, and kill so many attacking soldiers, that the invasion would fail. Even though the *Luftwaffe* had greatly outnumbered the Royal Air Force in 1940, it had been defeated in the Battle of Britain, and Hitler had been forced to call off his planned invasion. Now the Allied air forces had the same kind of numerical superiority over the Germans. But unless they could do better than Goering and the *Luftwaffe* had done four years earlier, Operation OVERLORD might end in a bloody defeat.

Under Eisenhower and Tedder were three Allied airmen who were responsible for leading the fight against the *Luftwaffe* and for supporting the ground and naval forces in their assaults against the German coast defenses. These were: British Air Chief Marshal Sir Trafford Leigh-Mallory, American Lieutenant General Carl Spaatz, and British Air Chief Marshal Sir Arthur T. Harris.

Under Eisenhower, Leigh-Mallory was the commander in chief of all of the tactical air forces assigned to OVERLORD. By June, 1944, these totaled more than ten thousand first-line planes: fighters, light and medium bombers, reconnaissance and photographic planes, and transports. More than half of these were American aircraft, the remainder belonged to the Royal Air Force. In the months before June these tactical air units made many short-range attacks and reconnaissance missions across the English Channel from England, but their principal job was to get ready for the intense activity that would begin on "D-Day" — the day of the actual landing.

Some of the Royal Air Force planes assembled for the Normandy invasion. The stripes on the planes indicate that they are part of the invasion forces.

General Spaatz and Air Marshal Harris were the commanders of the American and British heavy, strategic, bombing forces. They were controlled by the British-American Combined Chiefs of Staff, and were not placed directly under the command of Eisenhower. They were, however, instructed to give Eisenhower all possible assistance, and most of their long-range bombing attacks in early 1944 were planned to help prepare for the great invasion of western Europe.

Ninth Air Force Douglas A-20's attack defenses on the French coast.

The Role of Strategic Air Power

In January, 1944, the United States Army Air Forces created the U.S. Strategic Air Forces in Europe, under General Spaatz. This consisted of the American Eighth Air Force based in England, and the Fifteenth Air Force in Italy. By June, 1944, the U.S. Strategic Air Forces in Europe totaled more than three thousand heavy bombers and sixteen hundred long-range fighters. While the American strategic bombers were carrying out their daylight attacks, the Royal Air Force's Bomber Command of Air Chief Marshal Harris continued its devastating nighttime raids of German industrial areas. The British blows were coordinated with those of the Americans, to prevent the Germans from making quick recoveries from either the daylight or night attacks. By this time Bomber Command consisted of nearly fifteen hundred heavy bombers.

The Combined Bomber Offensive of the strategic air forces did much to reduce the effectiveness of German fighter defenses of occupied France. The American bombers and their fighter escorts shot down so many *Luftwaffe* fighters that the Germans had a hard time replacing the pilots who were killed or disabled. Also, German air operations were greatly hampered by vigorous Allied attacks against oil refineries and synthetic oil plants. By an intensive and well-planned production effort, under Albert Speer, German Minister of Armaments Production, the Germans replaced all of the fighter planes they had lost, but they had a hard time training enough pilots for their new fighters. The older *Luftwaffe* pilots had gone through a long series of training flights, but with oil and gasoline now so scarce in Germany, the new young pilots were unable to make enough training flights to prepare them properly for actual fighting. These half-trained pilots were quickly shot down by the American bombers and

41

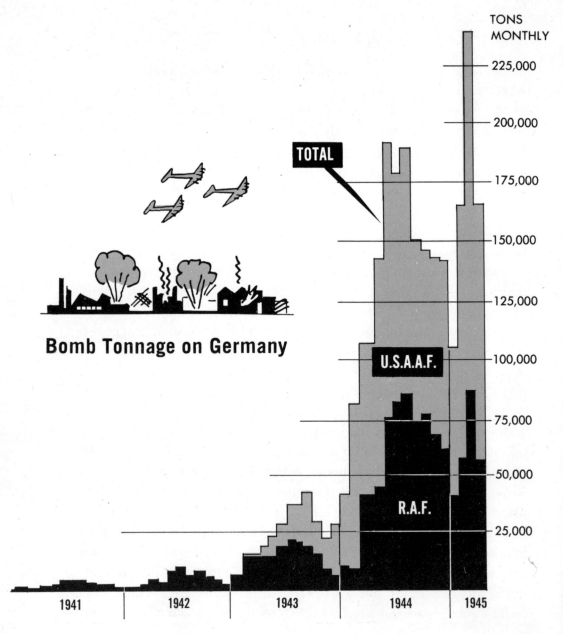

TONS MONTHLY

225,000
200,000
175,000
150,000
125,000
100,000
75,000
50,000
25,000

TOTAL

U.S.A.A.F.

R.A.F.

Bomb Tonnage on Germany

1941   1942   1943   1944   1945

fighters. This created a vicious cycle, in which the Germans had to use more precious fuel for partial training of more young fighter pilots, who were soon shot down because they did not have enough training.

The Germans had to keep most of their fighter pilots — and particularly their best ones — for the defense of Germany itself against the Combined Bomber Offensive. This meant that when the Allies began to carry out bombing raids over France in direct preparation for the invasion, the German fighter forces opposing them were quite weak. It was not long before the *Luftwaffe* defenses of northern France were almost completely destroyed.

In May and early June, most of the British and American long-range strategic bombers were joining Leigh-Mallory's fighters and bombers in an intensive assault to "isolate the battlefield" in the planned invasion area. Allied planes bombed railroad lines, roads, bridges, and communications centers. They also attacked German military installations and prevented German ground forces from moving at all during daylight hours. To keep the defenders from knowing the exact place where the landings were planned, the Allied bombers ranged over all of northern France, and the Germans, with their air power depleted, could do nothing to stop them.

Air Support Over the Beaches

IN THE EARLY MORNING HOURS of June 6, 1944, French peasants and German garrison troops in northwestern Normandy were awakened by a continuous, shattering roar. The almost unbearable racket continued for more than an hour as hundreds of low-flying airplanes, wave after wave of them, passed overhead. When the last wave had passed, most of those who had been awakened went back to sleep — briefly — thinking that this was just one more Allied air raid. Actually, it was something very different.

A Douglas C-47 tows a British Horsa-type glider loaded with American infantry to reinforce paratroopers dropped behind Nazi lines in France, June 6, 1944.

U.S. AIR FORCE PHOTO

At 2:00 A.M. paratroopers of the British 6th and the American 82nd and 101st airborne divisions had started to drop on French soil, a few miles behind the German coastal defenses. The Americans landed near Carentan, the British near Caen. Operation OVER-LORD had begun; the paratroopers were the spearhead of the greatest invasion ever attempted.

While the airborne soldiers were still assembling in the dark and beginning to exchange shots with surprised Germans, the roar of more planes could be heard coming across the Channel from England. At 3:14 A.M. a hail of bombs began to descend on the German fortifications along the beaches. For nearly three hours a tremendous, ear-splitting, devastating aerial bombardment all but drowned out the noise of hundreds upon hundreds of planes overhead.

Paratroopers drop into France on D-Day.

IMPERIAL WAR MUSEUM, LONDON

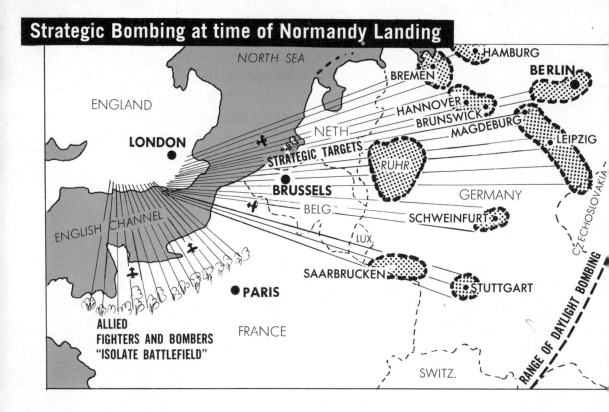

Strategic Bombing at time of Normandy Landing

NORTH SEA

HAMBURG

BREMEN

BERLIN

ENGLAND

HANNOVER
BRUNSWICK

NETH

MAGDEBURG

LEIPZIG

LONDON

STRATEGIC TARGETS

RUHR

BRUSSELS

GERMANY

ENGLISH CHANNEL

BELG.

SCHWEINFURT

LUX.

SAARBRUCKEN

STUTTGART

PARIS

CZECHOSLOVAKIA

ALLIED
FIGHTERS AND BOMBERS
"ISOLATE BATTLEFIELD"

FRANCE

RANGE OF DAYLIGHT BOMBING

SWITZ.

Shortly after sunrise, just before 6:00 A.M., the air bombardment ceased. French civilians and German soldiers peeked cautiously from their shelters toward the sky, then burrowed deep again as another infernal, thunderous tornado of fire swept over the beaches — this time from hundreds of Allied naval vessels gathering off the coast. About half an hour later the naval gunfire stopped abruptly.

The aerial and naval bombardments had wrecked many of the German coastal fortifications; the surviving defenders were stunned and deafened by the terrible ordeal they had experienced. But despite terror and shock, alert German lookouts kept to their posts and soon saw a great line of boats, stretching for miles, speeding toward the shore. German coast defense guns had just begun to open fire on these landing craft when another wave of airplanes swept over the beaches. This time it was the U.S. Army Air Force and the Royal Air Force fighter planes, dropping small bombs and strafing the beaches and forts with machine-gun bullets. Every time a German gun fired, it attracted a flock of deadly fighter planes.

While the German defenders were kept busy trying to fend off the aerial attack, the first waves of landing craft reached the shore, and Allied soldiers began to swarm across the beaches. Now the Allied fighter planes had to lift their fire to avoid shooting down their own ground troops who were moving up on the German coastal forts. Leaving the soldiers to continue their deadly short-range land battle, the Allied fighters swept inland from the beaches, seeking out German artillery emplacements, and attacking any moving troops they could see on the roads or in the fields of Normandy.

Throughout this terrible day, and the ones that followed, Allied fighter planes came in never-ending waves across the Channel, attacking any targets they could see, dropping bombs and strafing German strongpoints to which they were directed by radio messages from British or American ground troops. At the same time, the light and medium bombers of the tactical air forces and the heavy bombers of the strategic air forces struck further inland against roads, railroads, bridges and all German troop concentrations.

There was no effective German air opposition. The Allied air forces had established complete domination over the skies of Normandy. Assisted by direct air support, and by the effective "isolation of the battlefields," the invading soldiers soon were securely established in a beachhead seventy-five miles long and twenty miles deep. Thanks to air power, OVERLORD had been successful.

Air War Over Western Europe

Breakout from Normandy

WHILE ALLIED GROUND SOLDIERS pushed inland from the Normandy beaches, Allied engineers began to build airfields inside the beachhead. Within the first week of the invasion three of these airfields were in operation, and more were being built. Fighter-bombers flew across the English Channel into these new bases from which they could give more and better support to the frontline troops.

Although the Germans resisted fiercely, the Allies steadily enlarged their Normandy beachhead during June and July. This was due largely to the direct support given the ground troops by tactical air forces, but even more to the sweeps of bombers and fighters over northern France. These great aerial assaults prevented the Germans from moving either by road or railroad during daylight hours, seriously interfering with the arrival of German reinforcements to Normandy. Meanwhile, more Allied ground and air units kept arriving from England in preparation for a major attack to break through the surrounding German lines.

The great attack took place on July 25, near Saint-Lo. It began with a gigantic air strike by 1,500 heavy strategic bombers of the Eighth Air Force, plus 400 medium bombers and 550 fighter-bombers of the tactical air forces. In three hours, over 4,700 tons of bombs were dropped in a section of the German lines only 7,000 yards wide and 3,000 yards deep. A few bombs from this "carpet bombing" fell inside the American lines and caused some casualties. Most landed in the target area, pulverizing the defenses, killing, wounding, or stunning most of the German troops there.

Despite constant punishment from air attacks, the Germans rushed reinforcements to the devastated area and fought fiercely, but American ground forces poured through the gap. In a few days they had made a complete breakthrough, and the tanks of General George S. Patton's Third American Army drove southward. The Germans tried to cut off the American spearheads with one desperate counterattack, but combined Allied ground and air action threw them back in disastrous defeat.

In the days that followed, British and American ground forces surrounded and captured large portions of the *Wehrmacht,* while Allied air forces slashed at the columns of retreating German troops trying to make their way to eastern France and Germany. In three days in mid-August, about seventy thousand German troops were killed and captured. They were learning how it feels to be on the receiving end of *blitzkrieg.*

As the German troops continued to retreat eastward, the British and American armies pursued them without letup, and Allied planes harassed them. At the same time, relentless sweeps of General O.P. Weyland's 19th Tactical Air Command, supporting General Patton, cut off and prevented the escape of Germans south of the Loire River. Weyland had intended these sweeps merely to protect the right flank of the rapidly advancing Third Army. He was surprised when the isolated Germans insisted on surrendering to his representative. This was probably the first time that ground troops had ever surrendered to air forces.

The V-Bombs

AMONG THE IMPORTANT OBJECTIVES of the Allied ground troops, as they raced eastward from the Normandy Beachhead, were German missile-launching sites along the English Channel coast of France.

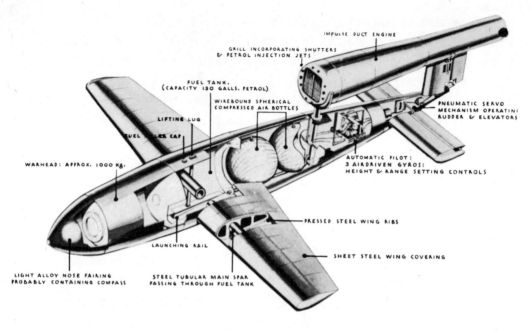

Diagram of a V-1 flying bomb.

IMPULSE DUCT ENGINE

GRILL INCORPORATING SHUTTERS
& PETROL INJECTION JETS

FUEL TANK,
(CAPACITY 130 GALLS. PETROL)

WIREBOUND SPHERICAL
COMPRESSED AIR BOTTLES

PNEUMATIC SERVO
MECHANISM OPERATING
RUDDER & ELEVATORS

LIFTING LUG

FUEL FILLER CAP

AUTOMATIC PILOT:
3 AIRDRIVEN GYROS:
HEIGHT & RANGE SETTING CONTROLS

WARHEAD: APPROX. 1000 Kg.

PRESSED STEEL WING RIBS

SHEET STEEL WING COVERING

LAUNCHING RAIL

LIGHT ALLOY NOSE FAIRING
PROBABLY CONTAINING COMPASS

STEEL TUBULAR MAIN SPAR
PASSING THROUGH FUEL TANK

IMPERIAL WAR MUSEUM

One of the V-1 flying bombs launched by Germany against England.

IMPERIAL WAR MUSEUM, LONDON

For more than two months the Germans had been firing new, long-range missiles at England, despite frequent air attacks against these sites by Allied bombers. The contest between Allied airplanes and German missiles had started almost a year earlier.

During 1943 Hitler had threatened to use "secret weapons" against the Allies. At the same time, British spies in Europe had begun to report that German scientists were perfecting long-range rocket weapons, and Allied reconnaissance planes had brought back air photographs showing unusual German activities on the coast of the Baltic Sea.

For some time German scientists and military men had been testing new weapons at an experimental station on the island of Peenemunde on the Baltic coast of north Germany. One of these weapons was a jet-propelled, pilotless airplane, called the V-1. This missile carried almost two thousand pounds of explosives in its nose, and could fly more than one hundred miles at a speed of more than four hundred miles per hour — slightly faster than the fastest British Spitfires and American P-51's. The Germans had expected that this weapon would be ready for use against England in late 1943.

Hitler had also hoped that an even more powerful missile would be ready a few months later. This was a rocket which the Germans called the V-2. Propelled by a liquid oxygen fuel, it could carry a ton of explosives more than two hundred miles at a speed of more than three thousand miles per hour. This V-2 rocket was the first modern missile, pointing the way to postwar intercontinental ballistic missiles, and to rockets which would eventually orbit the earth and penetrate deep into outer space.

Before the Germans were ready to use either of these long-range weapons against England, the British had struck at the experimental station. In August, 1943, the Royal Air Force had staged a great

51

V-1 launching site being constructed at Yvrendi in northern France November, 1943.

Diagram of a completed V-1 launching site at Maisoncelle, France.

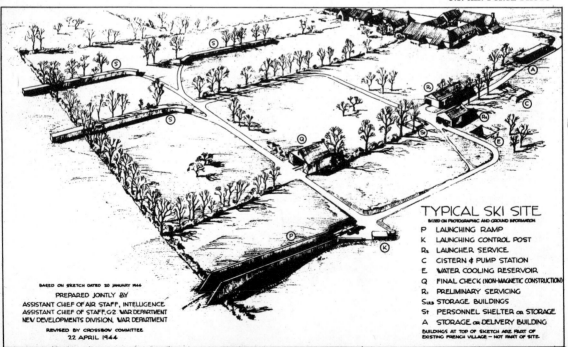

TYPICAL SKI SITE
BASED ON PHOTOGRAPHIC AND GROUND INFORMATION

P   LAUNCHING RAMP
K   LAUNCHING CONTROL POST
R₂ LAUNCHER SERVICE
C   CISTERN & PUMP STATION
E   WATER COOLING RESERVOIR
Q   FINAL CHECK (NON-MAGNETIC CONSTRUCTION)
R₁ PRELIMINARY SERVICING
S₁ₐ STORAGE BUILDINGS
St PERSONNEL SHELTER or STORAGE
A   STORAGE or DELIVERY BUILDING
BUILDINGS AT TOP OF SKETCH ARE PART OF
EXISTING FRENCH VILLAGE - NOT PART OF SITE.

BASED ON SKETCH DATED 20 JANUARY 1944
PREPARED JOINTLY BY
ASSISTANT CHIEF OF AIR STAFF, INTELLIGENCE
ASSISTANT CHIEF OF STAFF, G-2 WAR DEPARTMENT
NEW DEVELOPMENTS DIVISION, WAR DEPARTMENT
REVISED BY CROSSBOW COMMITTEE
22 APRIL 1944

raid on Peenemunde, causing severe damage and delaying the development of both V-1 and V-2 for several months. In the spring of 1944, Allied planes had begun to bomb newly constructed launching sites on the French coast. This had still further delayed German preparations.

On June 13, 1944, however, the first V-1 missiles struck England. During the next few months the Germans fired over eight thousand of these flying bombs across the Channel, most of them against London. Although many of these bombs caused great damage and created much uneasiness among Londoners, they did not seriously affect the British war effort. Furthermore, the Royal Air Force's Fighter Command discovered that, with the assistance of radar, their Spitfires could frequently intercept these missiles. About half of the V-1's were shot down by antiaircraft guns or fighter planes before they reached London or other populated areas.

One of the most dramatic incidents of the British defensive effort against the V-1 occurred on August 4, 1944. A new and experimental British jet fighter plane caught up with one of the flying bombs. The Royal Air Force pilot slipped his wingtip under the wing of the V-1, then flipped it over. The bomb plummeted harmlessly into an open field.

The first V-2 was launched against England on September 8, 1944. Because of their terrific speed, these rockets could not be intercepted by any existing plane or antiaircraft gun. During the next few weeks, however, Allied ground armies advancing from Normandy overran most of the German V-1 and V-2 bases in France and Belgium.

The Germans continued to fire V-2's against England from launching sites in Holland. Allied bombers hammered these bases constantly, however, preventing the Germans from ever making a really

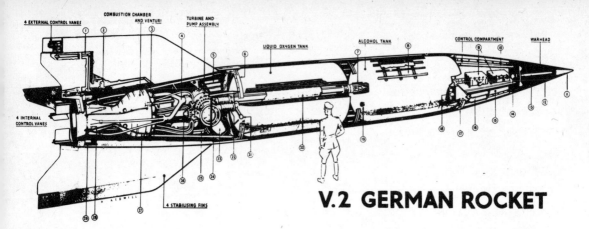

4 EXTERNAL CONTROL VANES — COMBUSTION CHAMBER AND VENTURI — TURBINE AND PUMP ASSEMBLY — LIQUID OXYGEN TANK — ALCOHOL TANK — CONTROL COMPARTMENT — WARHEAD

4 INTERNAL CONTROL VANES

4 STABILISING FINS

V.2 GERMAN ROCKET

1 CHAIN DRIVE TO EXTERNAL CONTROL VALVES.

2 ELECTRIC MOTOR.

3 BURNER CUPS.

4 ALCOHOL SUPPLY FROM PUMP.

5 AIR BOTTLES.

6 REAR JOINT RING AND STRONG POINT FOR TRANSPORT.

7 SERVO-OPERATE ALCOHOL OUTLET VALVE.

8 ROCKET SHELL CONSTRUCTION.

9 RADIO EQUIPMENT.

10 PIPE LEADING FROM ALCOHOL TANK TO WARHEAD.

11 NOSE PROBABLY FITTED WITH NOSE SWITCH OR OTHER DEVICE FOR OPERATING WARHEAD FUZE.

12 CONDUIT CARRYING WIRES TO NOSE OR WARHEAD.

13 CENTRAL EXPLORER TUBE.

14 ELECTRIC FUZE FOR WARHEAD.

15 PLYWOOD FRAME.

16 NITROGEN BOTTLES.

17 FRONT JOINT RING AND STRONG POINT FOR TRANSPORT.

18 PITCH AND AZIMUTH GYROS.

19 ALCOHOL FILLING POINT

20 DOUBLE WALLED ALCOHOL DELIVERY PIPE TO PUMP.

21 OXYGEN FILLING POINT.

22 CONCERTINA CONNECTIONS.

23 HYDROGEN PEROXIDE TANK.

24 TUBULAR FRAME HOLDING TURBINE AND PUMP ASSEMBLY.

25 PERMANGANATE TANK (GAS GENERATOR UNIT BEHIND THIS TANK).

26 OXYGEN DISTRIBUTOR FROM PUMP

27 ALCOHOL PIPES FOR SUBSIDIARY COOLING.

28 ALCOHOL INLET TO DOUBLE WALL.

29 ELECTRO HYDRAULIC SERVO MOTORS.

intensive missile assault on England. About 1,250 V-2's were fired at England between September 8, 1944, and March 27, 1945. Between them, the V-1's and the V-2's killed about 9,000 people in England, and seriously injured nearly 24,000 more.

When the V-1's could no longer reach England, the Germans began to fire them against targets in France and Belgium. Between October, 1944, and the end of March, 1945, they launched nearly ten thousand more of these flying bombs. They also fired nearly two thousand V-2's against Allied activities in Belgium and France. Their main target was the seaport of Antwerp, which had become the main supply base for General Eisenhower's armies in Europe. Antwerp suffered more than thirty thousand casualties from both types of missiles.

GERMAN V-2 ROCKET LAUNCHING

1) *German V-2 rocket being wheeled to its launching site on a Meiler wagon,
   which will later serve as a launching platform.*
2) *The rocket begins to rise to firing position.*
3) *The rocket in firing position.*
4) *The rocket takes off.*

Air-Ground Cooperation

DURING THE LATTER PART OF 1944, Allied ground forces closed in on Germany from three directions. In the east, Russian armies smashed through the Baltic States, Poland, and the Balkan countries. From the south, British, American, and other Allied forces advanced slowly through Italy. To the west, General Eisenhower's armies had reconquered most of France, parts of Belgium and Holland, and actually had a foothold on German soil at Aachen.

These Allied ground successes were greatly aided by tactical air support. As we have seen, outside of Germany itself, the *Luftwaffe* was unable to challenge Allied control of the skies. And even over Germany, the Allied strategic bombers and fighters were now seldom attacked by German fighters. The *Luftwaffe* did not have enough planes and trained pilots to attempt large-scale air battles against the powerful Allied air forces. The Allied tactical air units no longer had to worry about the first task of air support. They had overwhelming air superiority.

For this reason, during the last year of the war, Allied tactical pilots devoted themselves almost entirely to attacking targets on the ground. Only occasionally did they have a chance to fight in the sky against German hit-and-run raiders.

The Allies had learned lessons in North Africa that proved equally useful in the war in Europe. Allied air strikes against railroads, roads, and bridges made it very difficult for the Germans to reinforce their fighting fronts, but it was impossible for attacking air units to stop all ground activity completely. Supply and troop movements were always possible at night, or during bad weather, when pilots could not see the ground. Even in clear daylight a few trucks, cars, tanks, and foot soldiers could always sneak past the Allies by using wooded

The Ulm rail yards, Ulm, Germany, which supplied the German fighting Eighth Army near Karlsruhe, were half demolished by the Eighth Air Force in December, 1944. U.S. AIR FORCE PHOTO

roads and taking advantage of times when no planes were overhead. But during late 1944, and early 1945, Allied air forces came very close to "isolating the battlefield."

At the same time, large numbers of Allied fighter-bombers were always ready to assist the ground troops in attacks against stubborn German field defenses. Working in close cooperation with artillery, the planes would drop explosive or incendiary bombs on the German trenches and emplacements. Then they would spray the area with strafing machine-gun fire. Without these air strikes the ground advances would have been much slower, and many more Allied soldiers would have been killed or wounded.

This kind of air attacks against ground targets was particularly important in support of airborne forces, because when paratroops landed behind the enemy lines, they could bring no artillery of their own with them. But even with assistance from tactical aircraft, isolated airborne units could sometimes be overwhelmed by the enemy.

The Airborne Operations

Before the Normandy invasion, the largest airborne operation of the war had been the German two-division assault on Crete. The Germans had used small airborne units in their other early *blitzkrieg* victories, and the Allies had dropped a few paratroops in their operations in North Africa, Sicily, and Italy. After OVERLORD, in August, 1944, several airborne battalions had played an important part in the Allied landings on the coast of southern France.

The next big airborne activity came in September, 1944. At that time the Allies were approaching the frontiers of Germany, and German resistance was becoming ever more desperate. General Eisenhower and General Montgomery knew that the Germans might be able to stop the Allied advance at the Rhine River, and so they decided to try to seize the Rhine bridge at Arnhem, in Holland, by using airborne troops in a surprise attack. This was called Operation MARKET GARDEN.

By mid-September the leading British ground units were still in northern Belgium, thirty miles from Arnhem, held there by the Germans' skillful defense of the numerous streams and canals in this portion of the Low Countries. Between the front lines and the Lek (Lower Rhine) River at Arnhem lay two other broad rivers — the Maas (Lower Meuse) and the Waal (the main branch of the Rhine). The Allies decided that airborne units would have to seize the crossings over both of these rivers at the same time·the main drop was made at Arnhem.

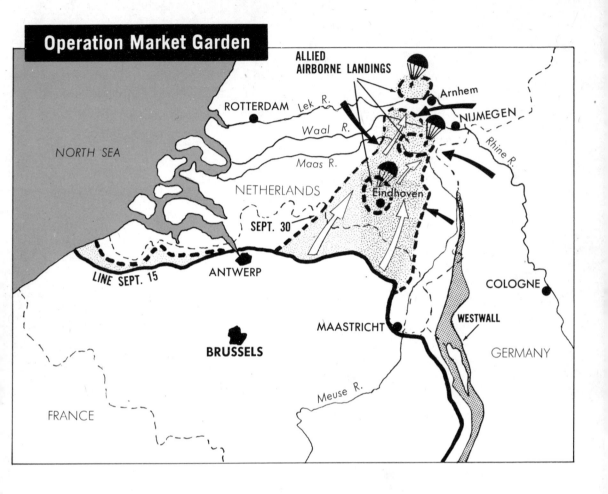

Operation Market Garden

On September 17, there began the largest airborne operation in history. Taking part were the American 82nd and 101st Airborne divisions, the British 1st Airborne Division, and the Polish Parachute Brigade. These were carried to their targets by 2,800 transport planes and 1,600 gliders. They were escorted by hundreds of Allied fighters. The British and Polish paratroops landed on the north bank of the Lek River, near Arnhem. The 101st Division landed near Eindhoven,

Planes of a troop carrier command return to base over a flooded section of Holland after dropping paratroops during landings of the Allied Airborne Army. The flooding of the Dutch lowlands was a desperate measure of defense by the Germans.   U.S. ARMY PHOTOGRAPH

to seize crossings over the waterways south of the Maas, while the 82nd Division dropped to capture the Maas and Waal bridges at Grave and Nijmegen.

It was a brilliantly planned, efficiently executed operation. All went well at first, though German resistance at Arnhem was heavier than expected. But on September 18, bad weather prevented most of the flights of reinforcements and supplies from reaching the airheads. The weather also kept Allied fighters from helping the paratroopers to fight off the fierce German ground counterattacks.

Despite desperate German resistance and the flooded countryside, British ground troops fought their way to and beyond the bridges which American airborne divisions had captured and held. But the German defenses stiffened south of Arnhem. The British and Polish paratroopers near Arnhem were surrounded and overwhelmed. A few fought their way to the south bank of the Lek and escaped, but most were killed or captured by the Germans. By sheer skill and stubbornness, and with considerable help from the weather, the Germans had completely disrupted the Allied operation.

The last airborne operation of the war in Europe took place on March 24, 1945. Once again the Allied objective was to gain control of a crossing over the Rhine River. This time, however, Allied troops were already at the riverbank, near Wesel, Germany, in great force. They had already begun to cross the river by the time the American 17th and British 6th Airborne divisions dropped a few miles further east. Combined ground, air, and airborne attacks quickly overcame German resistance. Allied armored spearheads began to dash eastward to bring about the final and complete defeat of Germany.

The Destruction of the *Luftwaffe*

Climax of the Strategic Air Offensive

AFTER ASSISTING General Eisenhower's armies in the breakout from the Normandy Beachhead, the Allied strategic air forces returned to their principal mission of destroying Germany's basic war-making capability. The principal efforts were directed against oil production and against the German transportation system, but the air forces attacked other important German industries, too: steel plants, electric power facilities, weapons factories, and all large industrial areas.

The blows against oil refineries and synthetic oil plants continued to have a disastrous effect upon the *Luftwaffe*. Lack of fuel reduced the training of new pilots still further. The Germans had to hoard their scanty fuel for use against only the most dangerous Allied air raids. The fuel shortage meant also that the tanks and trucks of the *Wehrmacht* could be used very infrequently; submarine warfare had to be drastically reduced in intensity. Thus the strategic air attacks against German oil production had immediate and direct effects upon the fighting capabilities of German land, sea, and air forces.

The blows against German road and railroad transportation systems were just as serious, though the impact was slightly less direct. All forms of industrial production were affected. Raw materials could not get to factories. Finished products — weapons, equipment, food, and supplies for fighting forces and the civilian population — could not reach the places where they were needed. By the spring of 1945, the German economy was close to complete collapse. Most large German cities were smoking ruins. The Allied air attacks had killed at least 100,000 Germans, and injured many thousands more.

By April the advances of the Allied ground forces into Germany had come close to overrunning the entire country. The strategic air forces had practically run out of targets. The few German factories that were still producing were now within range of the medium bombers and fighter bombers of the tactical air forces. Air Chief Marshal Harris and General Spaatz therefore decided to use their heavy bombers in direct support of the onrushing British and American armies, in order to hasten the final overthrow of the German armed forces.

U.S. Eighth Air Force Liberators and Flying Fortresses bomb the oil refineries at Hamburg, Germany.

The Luftwaffe's *Last Efforts*

Despite its terrible losses, and despite the inexperience of most of its new pilots, the *Luftwaffe* fought vigorously in the defense of Germany in 1944 and early 1945. Occasionally the German fighters made violent attacks against the strategic raids of the Allied heavy bombers. Every once in a while a few German bombers would retaliate with hit-and-run raids against Allied airfields, military installations, and cities.

In early 1944, finding themselves unable to fight effectively against the P-51 fighters escorting the American daylight bombers, the leaders of the *Luftwaffe* had begun to concentrate their efforts on the development of new night fighters and night fighting techniques against the British raids. As a result, the British bombers suffered increasingly heavy losses, until the advance of Allied ground forces reduced the efficiency of the German early warning system, and cut down the number of bases suitable for night fighters. Furthermore, the German night fighter effort suffered from the fuel shortage.

German scientists and airmen also paid increasing attention to the development of their new jet fighter planes. In early 1945, increasing numbers of Messerschmitt 262 twin-jet fighters began to seriously alarm the Allies, who had not made such rapid advances in jet aircraft, and whose fighters could not match the performance of the new Messerschmitts.

But the German switch to jet fighters came too late to affect the outcome of the air war. Superior numbers of conventional planes, and the superior training and operational efficiency of the Allied pilots — who had no fuel shortage to worry about — prevented the jet Messerschmitts from seriously threatening Allied air superiority.

The *Luftwaffe* suffered its final, crushing blow in four days between March 21 and 24, 1945. As Field Marshal Montgomery's armies were preparing to cross the Rhine near Wesel, Allied strategical and tactical air force planes flew a total of 42,000 sorties over Germany. These missions were flown from bases in England, France, Belgium, and Italy. More than 1,200 heavy bombers of the U.S. Eighth Air Force smashed all the German jet air bases within range of Wesel, while medium bombers and fighter-bombers struck at all other German air installations.

The war lasted only six weeks more after this tremendous air effort. Allied ground forces quickly overran the *Luftwaffe* bases. By May 8, 1945, when the remaining German armed forces surrendered, the once-mighty *Luftwaffe* had ceased to exist.

Index

Aachen, 56
Afrika Korps, 9
Airborne operations, 58-61
Air-ground cooperation, 10-18, 56-58
Algeria, 13, 16
Antiaircraft defenses, 21, 28, 30, 32, 53
Antwerp, and V-bombs, 54
Arnhem, 58-61
Arnold, Henry H., 23

Balkans, 9, 56
Ball-bearing factory, Schweinfurt, 32-35
Baltic Seacoast, 51
Baltic States, 56
Battle of Britain, 1, 19, 23, 38
Belgium, 53, 54, 56
Benghazi, 27
Berlin, 7, 34
Bizerte, 13
Bomber Command, R.A.F., 19-36, 40
Bombsights, 24
B-17's ("Flying Fortresses"), 24, 27-28, 32
B-24's ("Liberators"), 24, 27-28, 32
Bulgaria, 28

Caen, 44
Carentan, 44
Casablanca, 13
Casablanca Conference, 36
Churchill, Winston, 23, 36
Cologne, 23
Combined Bomber Offensive, 40-43
Coningham, Arthur, 10, 18
Crete, 9, 58

"D-Day," 38. *See also* Operation
    OVERLORD
Desert Air Force, R.A.F., 7-18

Egypt, 9
Eighth Air Force, U.S., 24-26, 27, 34-35, 40,
    48, 64
Eighth Army, British, 10
82nd Airborne Division, U.S., 44, 59-60
Eindhoven, 59

Eisenhower, Dwight D., 13, 16, 18, 36-39,
    54, 56, 58, 61
El Alamein, 10, 13, 16
El Guettar, 16
England, and V-bombs, 51-54. *See also*
    Battle of Britain

Faid, 16
Fifteenth Air Force, U.S., 34-35, 40
First Air Fleet, German, 1
1st Airborne Division, British, 59
Fourth Air Fleet, German, 1
Fredendall, Lloyd, 16
French Algeria, 13
French Morocco, 13

Galland, Adolf, 34
Germany (*Also throughout*):
    British raids on, 19-23
    combined bomber offensive against, 26-36
Goering, Hermann, 20, 34, 38
Grave, 60
Greece, 9, 28

Harris, Arthur T., 24, 38, 39, 40, 62
Hitler, *throughout*
Holland, 53-54, 56, 58-61
Hurricanes, 7

"Isolation of the Battlefield" doctrine, 12, 43,
    47, 57
Italy, 36

Japan, 23
Jet fighter planes, 64

Kasserine Pass, 16
Keller, Alfred, 1
Kesselring, Albert, 1

Leigh-Mallory, Trafford, 38, 43
Lek River, 58, 59, 61
Lend-lease, to Russia, 4, 7
Libya, 9, 27
Loehr, Alexander, 1

Loire River, 49
London, and V-bombs, 53
Luftwaffe, throughout

Maas River, 58, 60
Malta, 9
Mareth, 16
Messerschmitts, 9, 34, 64
Middle East, 7
Missiles, 49-54
Montgomery, Bernard L., 10, 58, 64
Moscow, 4, 7
Night bombing, 21
Night fighting techniques, 63-64
19th Tactical Air Command, 49
Ninth Air Force, U.S., 24, 27
Nijmegen, 60
Normandy, 36-49, 61
North Africa, 7-18

Oil Refineries, Ploesti, 27-32
101st Airborne Division, U.S., 44, 59-60
Operation MARKET GARDEN, 58
Operation OVERLORD, 36-47
Oran, 13

Paratroops, 13, 44-45, 58-61
Patton, George S., 49
Pearl Harbor, 23, 24
Peenemunde, 51, 53
P-51's ("Mustangs"), 34, 35, 51, 63
Ploesti, 27-32
Poland, 56
Polish Parachute Brigade, 59
Portal, Charles, 23

Radar, 21, 28, 53
Red Army, 1-7, 56
Rhine River, 58, 61, 64
Rocket weapons, 49-54
Romania, 28
Rommel, Erwin, 9-10, 13, 16, 18
Roosevelt, Franklin D., 23, 36
Rouen, 24

Royal Air Force, *throughout*
Royal Air Force Bomber Command, 40
Russia, invasion of, 1-7

Saint-Lo, 48
Schweinfurt, 32-35
Second Air Fleeet, German, 1
17th Airborne Division, U.S., 61
Sicily, 36
6th Airborne Division, British, 44, 61
Sixth Army, German, 4-5
Southern Army Group, German, 1
Soviet air force, 2-3, 4, 7. *See also* Russia
Soviet Union, *see* Russia
Spaatz, Carl, 24, 38, 39, 40, 62
Speer, Albert, 40
Spitfires, 7, 51, 53
Stalingrad, 4-5
Strategic Air Offensive, 19-36, 61-62
Strategic air power, role of, 40-43
Stukas, 9
Suez Canal, 9

Tebessa, 16
Tedder, Arthur W., 10, 18, 36-38
Third Army, U. S., 49
Tobruk, 9
Tunisia, 13-18, 36
Twelfth Air Force, U. S., 24

U. S. Army Air Force, *throughout*
U.S.S.R., *see* Russia

V-bombs, 49-54
Vichy-French, 13
Von Arnim, D. J., 13-14

Waal River, 58, 60
Wehrmacht, throughout
Wesel, 61, 64
Western desert, air power in, 7-18
Western Europe, air war in, 48-61
Weyland, O. P., 49
Wilhelmshaven, 26